GOLDEN RETRIEVERS

by Mary Ellen Klukow

D1531158

AMICUS | AMICUS INK

Amicus High Interest and Amicus Ink are published by Amicus
P.O. Box 1329, Mankato, MN 56002
www.amicuspublishing.us

Library of Congress Cataloging-in-Publication Data
Names: Klukow, Mary Ellen, author.
Title: Golden retrievers / by Mary Ellen Klukow.
Description: Mankato, Minnesota : Amicus/Amicus Ink, [2020] | Series:
  Favorite dog breeds | Audience: K to Grade 3. | Includes index.
Identifiers: LCCN 2018025936 (print) | LCCN 2018031493 (ebook) | ISBN
  9781681517391 (pdf) | ISBN 9781681516578 (library binding) | ISBN
  9781681524436 (paperback)
Subjects: LCSH: Golden retriever--Juvenile literature.
Classification: LCC SF429.G63 (ebook) | LCC SF429.G63 K58 2020 (print) |
  DDC 636.752/7--dc23
LC record available at https://lccn.loc.gov/2018025936

Photo Credits: Shutterstock/Irina oxilixo Danilova cover; iStock/GlobalP 2, 8–9; Shutterstock/Volodymyr Burdiak 5; iStock/vbacarin 6–7; iStock/ photodeti 9; Shutterstock/MirasWonderland 9; Alamy/Tierfotoagentur 10–11; iStock/Figure8Photos 13; AP/D Fahleson/Houston Chronicle 14–15; iStock/Photology1971 16–17; 123rf/Susan Richey-Schmitz 18; Shutterstock/Susan Schmitz 18; Alamy/Blue Jean Images 20–21; Shutterstock/Africa Studio 22–23

Editor: Alissa Thielges
Designer: Ciara Beitlich
Photo Researcher: Holly Young

Printed in the United States of America

HC 10 9 8 7 6 5 4 3 2 1
PB 10 9 8 7 6 5 4 3 2 1

TABLE OF CONTENTS

A HAPPY DOG

Thump! A dog wags its tail. The dog is big and yellow. It has a long, fluffy tail. It's a Golden retriever! Goldens are known for being happy and silly. They are friendly and smart, too.

Furry Fact
Goldens are the third most popular breed in America. They are second most popular in Canada.

DOUBLE COAT

All Goldens are yellow. Some are lighter in color. Others are darker. All have long fur coats. Their coats have two layers. The inner coat keeps them warm. The outer coat **repels** water.

HISTORY

Golden retrievers are from Scotland. Dudley Marjoribanks created this breed. He wanted a sweet dog that could hunt. It took him over 60 years to create the breed!

Furry Fact
Dudley mixed breeds like labs and setters to make Goldens.

HUNTING PARTNERS

Bang! A hunter shoots a bird. A Golden retriever brings the bird back to the hunter. This is what they were bred to do. Goldens are still trained for hunting.

HELPING OUT

Goldens have other jobs, too. Some are **service dogs**. They can lead blind people. Goldens are also used for **search-and-rescue**. They sniff through disaster areas. They find survivors.

FAMOUS GOLDENS

Some Goldens are famous. Bretagne, shown at left with her handler, helped rescue people after New York was attacked on September 11, 2001. The dogs in the *Air Bud* movies were also Goldens.

Furry Fact
Actor and singer Nick Jonas owns a Golden named Elvis!

PUPPIES

Golden retriever moms have
8 to 12 puppies in a **litter**.
Golden puppies grow quickly.
They need chew toys. The toys
help when the puppies' teeth
are growing.

TRAINING

Puppies grow up. They need to be trained. Goldens are easy to train. They are smart. They love to make people happy. They especially love eat treats!

FAMILY DOGS

Golden retrievers make great pets. People love their beautiful coats and sweet personalities. Goldens love to cuddle and play. They are part of the family.

HOW DO YOU KNOW IT'S A GOLDEN RETRIEVER?

blocky head

brown eyes

feathery tail

long coat

WORDS TO KNOW

lab – a Labrador Retriever; another kind of dog breed created for hunting

litter – a group of puppies all born at the same time from the same mother

repel – to keep something away

search-and-rescue – finding survivors of disasters so that they can be saved

service dog – a dog that assists people with disabilities

setter – a kind of dog breed created for hunting

LEARN MORE

Books

Duling, Kaitlyn. *Golden Retrievers.* Minneapolis: Jump!, 2018.

Frank, Sarah. *Golden Retrievers.* Minneapolis: Lerner Publications, 2019.

Gagne, Tammy. *Golden Retrievers.* Lake Elmo, Minn.: Focus Readers, 2018.

Websites

American Kennel Club: Golden Retriever
https://www.akc.org/dog-breeds/golden-retriever/

Animal Planet: Golden Retriever
http://www.animalplanet.com/breed-selector/dog-breeds/sporting/golden-retriever.html

INDEX